vision of a storm cloud

vision of a storm cloud

William Olsen

TRIQUARTERLY BOOKS
NORTHWESTERN UNIVERSITY PRESS

Evanston, Illinois

TriQuarterly Books
Northwestern University Press
Evanston, Illinois 60208-4210

Copyright © 1996 by William Olsen. Published 1996. All rights reserved.

Printed in the United States of America

ISBN 0-8101-5043-3 (cloth)
ISBN 0-8101-5044-1 (paper)

Library of Congress Cataloging-in-Publication Data

Olsen, William, 1954–
    Vision of a storm cloud / William Olsen.
        p. cm.
        ISBN 0-8101-5043-3 (cloth : alk. paper).—ISBN 0-8101-5044-1
    (paper : alk. paper)
        I. Title.
    PS3565.L822V57 1996
    811'.54—dc20   96-1876
                                                        CIP

The paper used in this publication meets the minimum requirements of the American
National Standard for Information Sciences—Permanence of Paper for Printed Library
Materials, ANSI Z39.48-1984.

Contents

Acknowledgments

Grateful acknowledgment is made to the following publications where some of these poems appeared, sometimes in different versions:

Antioch Review: "Brotherhood"
Crazyhorse: "Black Storm," "Happiness," "The Mysteries of the End"
The Gettysburg Review: "After Chartres," "Godlessness," "Reading Willa Cather"
The Indiana Review: "Bottomland," "At the Bus Stop"
The Iowa Review: "Fireworks," "Negative Confession"
Kenyon Review: "Cruising"
Michigan Quarterly Review: "Slow Train North"
New England Review: "Burning Houses"
The New Republic: "Big Language"
North American Review: "Choir Boys, Canterbury"
Paris Review: "Hereafter," "Old World Light"
Poetry Northwest: "The Human Brain," "Natural History," "Raptors"
Shenandoah: "The Oasis Motel"
Southern Review: "Heraclitus, Fragment 16"
TriQuarterly: "In the Time of Blithe Astonishments," "The Mist Nets"

"The Oasis Motel" was reprinted in *New American Poets of the Nineties* and in *Stepping Out: Poems about Hotels, Motels, Restaurants, and Bars.*

I'd like to thank Edward Hirsch, Lynda Hull (in memory), Richard Lyons, Susan Prospere, and David Wojahn for their help and encouragement. Special thanks to Nancy Eimers.

This book is for my mother and father.

i

Hereafter

How beautiful and vast and bright and empty
inside the quick-stop's inextinguishable glow.
Night has just begun to have its say.

The being in the checkered frock is free
to read the tabloids with a face like a broken window
and dream of being known and extraordinary

and towel the handprints off a jar of murdered jerky
and feel like a moviegoer in the very last row.
Night has just begun to have its say,

the pickled eggs seem older than all creation this Monday
or Tuesday or Wednesday, and years from now
how beautiful and vast and bright and empty

it may feel to be alive and mildly happy,
to walk between the aisles of a brand-new Stop-N-Go.
And when the century has its final say

may the tiny motels of our voices pray
that all the neon signs and wonders so
beautiful and vast and bright and empty
won't even have begun to have their say.

In the Time of Blithe Astonishments

An Eastern rattler stopped its swallowing—
my tin-cut shadow abiding over its
pleasantly shiny scales so close no evening vapor

could come between them. In the pink shed of an open mouth
a field mouse with its two showing paws
curled up to the spiraled end of the fiddle ferns
in their orchestral settlements—
its rib cage a miniature bellows at work,

the wind that ate the prophets
stumbling through the trees draped with the huge
snowflakes of spiderwebs—

my teeth couldn't look away. Frogs stranded in their ring of scum,
all but their eyes hiding,
letting in strawpiles of threshing-floor light,

Dante's flatterers up to their teeth in shit.
I had been taking in a blue-flag, the jawbone

of a cherub—

the horizon sinking upwards had clouds
thrown like spittle against it.
Something or
everything had doused the moon with gasoline
and set a match to it. For the smile of the highway.
The trucks have become bottomfeeders these evenings,

snapping up the mayflies in their headlights.
I couldn't look away until
the mouse actually gripped
the teeth of its punisher

for its foothold in this vast instant.

At the Bus Stop

Someone is sobbing into the ear of a flea,
someone coughs like a train passing the station by,
someone looks bored in this last of twenty worst centuries,
someone's hand jerks just like a hanging body jerks,
someone's mouth drools Dachau's own blue smoke,
someone and someone haven't exchanged a kiss
in seven thousand years, someone's plump little boy shrieks
at the greater disasters of his plumper father and mother.

Yet not one turns to his numberless crimes
to ask forgiveness, not one asks for more time—
there being so much more than we could ever
get over anyway on this bench of witnesses
who, so help us, though history is hopeless,

rise meekly to a little waiting bus.

Fireworks

1

A neighbor attached to his phone cord
follows its voice out across the porch to his easy chair.
Downstreet, bare-chested athletes aim skyrockets into a sugar maple
and are desolate again.
Out among the traffic that buried the town fathers
some hangover walking to work left his canvas glove
reaching out from the tarmac without a body to pull free.
Soon the fire-hazard bars will be
boarded up to keep the darkness in.
Like an extinct people
the dead cars resurrected

to a roar of transcended place.
A man with a mouthpiece to another world
is perishing in my thoughts and it doesn't even hurt.

2

These exclamations of longing,
sparklers in a child's hand,
used to be water and light and a little harmless dirt.
Someone to the north jabs a Roman candle
into his lawn, and how like smoke he is.
His kids scream narcs and pushers and Martians and Zarconians,
stand shirtless as in a frieze under Vesuvius,
as if they had been born and bathed clean

and named inside a hospital of fire.
They stare at the flames waiting for something
meteoric like the beginning to begin,
for a burning door to appear.

But here in this millennium my neighbor
who spends his evenings uttering his evenings away,
out loud, so every interested party
can hear how many friends afloat in calamitous seas
grasp for dear life to the frayed rope of his advice

pulls up in a Vega, steps out from
his car of the first magnitude,
mounts his porch, cradles a ringing telephone
and stands there talking while the neighborhood holds its ears—

3

What good can our small talk do America,
all our neighbors homeless in their feelings
behind snapshot windows the street lines up,
the newlyweds two houses down who scream
pots and pans and dishes as long as
one last joy remains intact?
They must sound even stranger
when in the blue snow of a television
they mouth each other's
shipyards and estuaries,
collapse to the tame
wilderness of the bed.
Excuse my patriotic
lust for endings, for
each stadium of earth

lost under a hoarse din of light
released by flames that never would be flames again.

4

I drift downstreet and take in the fireworks,
sidewalks gray with squibs and the spindrift of Black Cat scraps,
each star the punk-lit tip of a fuse.
The skinniest shirtless kid in the universe runs across
this street of transgressions and this street of reckonings
and this street of earthly returns—
across some kingdom come and gone he runs.
His show and tell's a garbage find, a balsa Cessna
with a bent propeller and a piece of lettuce
stuck to its plastic windshield like camouflage.
He places this gift
from some evicted household at my feet.
The simple cure for everything

would be to blow it up and let each paper bit
that used to be an airplane
break into many ashes. . . .
Instead, he runs across the street to another strange house.

5

All the stores on this our country's birthday
have barred their doors, in the antique shop window
the bridal gowns hold out their lace sleeves
to the stilettos of the willows.
Maybe seeing is a kind of copulation
from which issues
the nothingness of a night.
Maybe your eyes groped through

jail cells of fire,
and you could touch what you
saw and not destroy it, thank
God, or godlessness, for that, thank
the least leaves creeping out,

a strange gunpowder breath on your face,
embers like eyesight falling through the trees.

6

Each match flares up
its very own street,
illuminating kids who came from some place further
even than the darkened houses where nothing has changed for years.
And any sulfurous alien who wants to
is free as a burning witch to look off at a sky
given over to the Everlasting Yea of Aerials,
to dandelion fusillades in the gloom,
ribcages unlocking incendiary hearts.
So light the Frightened Birds,

The Howlers, the Flowering Plums,
The Tanks with their blue clouds of death smoke.
All prior attempts at happiness have failed.
These are no scared children
half-naked on the naked lawn of ashes
who walk armed into a defenseless night.

The Suicides

They'd want it said straightforward, untransformed
by the bee wafting like a dirigible
past the gutter half-ripped from peeling eaves

or by the kingbird gulping down the bee
or by the mud wasp that walks my kitchen window,
its forelegs clinging to a caterpillar,

feeding on the one helpless thing alike
in all of every edible moment like this one.
They'd want it said just what it is to have

to be so quiet they can't even tell us
it is not them we write about. We elegize their
agony into carrion. Besides, they're safe now,

while in a sense you kill yourself just reading this.
I think they'd want us to turn back
to our black ships before the next sacrifice

falls on the broken fields, and the black flies
settle on the knife wound and breed maggots
to defile the corpse with the ice-white

soon-to-be-winged children of the flies
that themselves die droning in farmyards round
the milk pails on spring days when the living

go their ways, and the lacewing dragonflies
lop in loose formations to drink from lady slippers,
lapping up nectar with hollow straws for tongues—

I look out on the marshland dreaming this.
In the world of the similes each suicide
groans the way Mishima groaned on camera,

his life-spirit tightroping a swaying highwire,
while a raging waterfall churns far below;
in this world, where I can't remember why

the kingbird's swoop gleamed like a bayonet,
the turntable turns, as the seasons turn,
and it is Brenda Lee singing "Emotions"

in 1963 in a soundproof studio
in Memphis, or Nashville, or Hollywood,
and through the shadows her voice just kills me,

*emotion, what are you doin', oh don't you know
you'll be my ruin?* Each feeling is a future little
angel rubbing its hands above the suicide

or each feeling *is* a little secret suicide,
dying by choice: Mishima's, Berryman's,
Romeo's, Juliet's, and closer to home,

elsewhere on the rungless ladder, Joe Bolton's,
my onetime friend who won't care what you think,
who can't care what you think, for here he goes:

into the afterlife of the dismal facts,
a million miles from earth or poetry . . .
the silence is obscene. In the movies

suicide is always better than dishonor,
more dramatic, a bigger box-office draw.
You place the .45 inside your mouth,

squeeze the trigger, your head slides down the wall,
a blossom of blood sentimentalizes the celluloid
afternoon light inside your abject flat

in Hell, Michigan, or Paradise the same
but beneath your window, where the orphans
of the dead pigeons bob along the parapet,

traffic flushes its tiny victims lifeward,
and light leaps suicidally from warehouse windows
but no it won't kill itself that easily,

for whatever terrible feelings the trucklights
are the carriers of below your priestly shortcut
go on fine without you, and the All

loosens a mouthful of smoke from your brainpan,
and there are no more kamikaze-ing songs,
and to say the joy or the danger should end

is beyond belief. So much for the movies.
Elsewhere my onetime friend is less than celluloid,
less than the voice of an answering service

when no one is home, though you wonder if someone
is, and simply chooses not to talk.
A second wasp creeps up the windowpane

as Brenda Lee's voice siphons to some canned end.
Her feelings seemed to choose her, but they didn't.
The kingbird is somewhere later, like a period

waiting for the sentence to end. Like a gunshot.
So each grief is a grievance, and to forget
is to forgive, and nothing is forgotten—

13

the marsh beyond me knells with straining toads
no matter if I listen or walk away,
the whole fucking world belting out one green slime song,

while glued to the white picket fence before me
are seventeen-year cicadas, a neat hole torn
through the same place of each carapace,

the winged nymphs having taken flight with everything
reckless and consequential and alive,
not with the voiceless papery husks

emptied of the rusty idea of death.
And we who are far enough away
from those self-dead to be the end,

the extreme of all small things,
have been erased a thousand times over.
They were once people we knew well enough.

Our future will have to tell them what they saw.

Burning Houses

Rain tapped on our windshields the one story
it never finishes on how each droplet
is absolutely wretched with its magnitudes,
each an ocean too small for Christ to walk across,
and if the first magnolia blossoms opened white and silent
into the streetlights, what crime had they done
to be condemned to this mugshot of a moment,
and isn't this what the moment invented us for?
Behind an emerald dashboard's calibrated privacies
I was one of a hundred drivers seated in rain,
but dry, all in a line of wide-eyed headlights.
Houselights burned through the rain like little lies,
soft childish embers throbbing through the shaken trees,
streetlights wound up in rain as if in packing twine,
a red light on a yellow stalk softly clicking green
just when we were getting used to giving in.
And the Safeway kind and bright in its neighborhood
like a match in the fog—
the fluorescent aisles for once some never-ending
threshold where shoppers seemed far off and benign,
and there I was already rolling toward the register
with food and sundries packaged inside some factory of fire,
and when I got home a neighbor's house was ablaze,
wallpaper ashes flapping companionably,
little nothings of transformation . . .
something thrown up from the furnace of a dream.

Memory incinerates the dismal facts,
but I remember the neighbor I'd never talked to
in a nurse's white smock standing beneath the whiter
coffee-cup blossoms of her front yard's precipitous magnolia,

ringed by a yard of hailstones all staring up.
She stood right there where you could put a hand to her,
she seemed more inconvenienced than anything else,
while a fireman from the other side of the smoke
and his yellow gloves that floated out from him
emerged with a Siamese cat with coals for eyes.
I sat on my porch with my forlorn grocery bag
watching a sprinkler throw superfluous lariats.
Then lightning put an end to any quiet
we think we could love because we have never
heard that quiet, but for one split second
the field across the street was specific with a few horses,
behind them the spilling lights of a city we all
believed, its discreet vacancies and habitations
peopled by the luminous citizens the city dreamed up,
each point in time and space simple and pointless,
behind which children played before TV
and men and women moved tongues in each other's mouths—

she watched her house burn almost uneventfully
down to charred walls, a brass bed and rampant piping
intestinal in the silence of rain-struck rooms
where something used to be happening to someone else.
The jets of water soon fell back, the ladders folded up,
and the firemen climbed into their truck and wheeled away
toward nothing that can be saved by calling out to it.
My neighbor could go to hell because nothing could be done:
her cat drenched spiky like a newborn chick
would make a little world for itself in a squad car,
the shoppers in the grocery store would keep sailing
their carts past cashiers with porchlights for faces,
the horses in their niche in the undergloom
ruminate upon their steaming pasture,
and everything take care of itself

through it all, through memory's antiseptic distances,
through this call to a nameless neighbor I obliquely
address to shelter myself
through the hail this past
perpetuates as long as it can,
through the smoldering regret that is the mere
ghost of astonishment—
she stood transfixed, solved of belonging
to much of anything, her memory
inviting her to enter the fire unscathed.

Choir Boys, Canterbury

It's raining outside their voices,
it's pouring tear gas on Tiananmen Square
and a baby is crying somewhere in the gloaming
behind the St. Thomas à Becket shrine. The pigeon
who dive-bombs the bald pate of the pastor gripping brass raptors
simply ascends from these pint-sized cherubs
as far from the dust as they will ever get.
I pretend to pray but sit inside a memory
of a train to St. Ives: a toy poodle plowing forth
a fat man along the Redruth station island,
teenagers smoking between cars, talking
about bloody good pensions,
tunnels peopled by our wry smiling reflections
dissolving to patchwork slopes and figurine horses,
as if by journeying so completely past
your running commentary on loss called loss
you can come onto some quiet pasture.

Whatever keeps me on my remembered train
secretly believes in eternity.
I see a cat and its silver bell emerge from the brush
in Axeminster with a field mouse in its mouth,
lying down beside somebody's green suitcase
like so much luggage with its dying toy
memory keeps knocking about. I see slopes shorn to stubble
by stone-cold sheep who get up like gravestones,
then the next tunnel blackens the gorgeous
scenery, and translucent passengers appear.
These choir boys have sung to history so long
you have to tear your miseries to shreds.
The evensong is everything we can walk outside—

the streetlights the heavens were unable to contain,
rain slipping through trees on pilgrim tourists
the rubble wears like carnations, each as much a threat
as the cry of someone being beaten
senseless in a small poor country.

After Chartres

One day a foreman took me up a flight of steel stairs to view
    the killing floor.
Dust flew up in a little skirt each time an electric prod
urged a pig onto the conveyor belt. The patience of Mary was every-
    where,
inside the machinery thinking out loud,
outside the sunrise rinsing Mercurochrome through the trees.
Pigs slopped up weeks of corn from troughs, tags of feed and shit
    hung from their legs and bellies,
and each came to the end of the line squealing
before the head shuddered frozen and the eyes turned upwards free
and a tired young man swept the blood into a drain with a smile
that smiled for us both or against us both,
against coming to the end of the exhilaration.
Hearing the shriek torn from the throat
assert its brief and bodiless cathedral, I think I got off
on one catharsis after another looking out for itself.
One day they will fasten my legs together with steel wire,
a metal hook on an overhead conveyor belt will yank me
off the table and out a back door
and pass my carcass through a ring of propane flame
to raze what hair the scalding butcher hose missed,
and in one refrigerated room, walls glazed so thick with live fat
you could write your name in it if you were not reading this,
a frowzy old woman will scrape my skull of its pituitary gland
and gently place the empty upon a crazy totemic stack
and there in a brainless skull will reign a light whole and roseate
like the light on hillsides when our train to Chartres came out
    of the tunnel
and it made us feel carnivorous and alive
to see those solid cows strung out on the hills.

Reapers left in the fields like escalators into Heaven.
We pilgrims came to see Art judge us, gray light a cool ash on our
    faces,
and the time it took the eyes to adjust to the stained glass
I harrowed for a memory of Paradise before the devil who had a
    gargoyle's face
really did push the damned into Hell with Piety's gold sceptre,
though even hell will end before we want it to.
I raked up this allegory of a middle-class white boy
suffocating fireflies in Mason jars
I buried beneath a plot of mother's Kentucky Wonders,
beyond all reach but the reach of memory,
a little light dying underground for the worms to steer by,
an afterglow to keep the ever-guessing thrill of death entranced.
I saw an ant lock the stained-glass wing of a fritillary
in its mandibles, with no way to fit that wing
through the hole to the undergloom where the Queen reigned.
The other drones would disassemble it, as the British National Trust
gingerly removed the York Minster's Great East Window, size of a
    tennis court,
during World War Two, so buzz bombs wouldn't shatter the
    beginning and end of the world.
Religious light always needed room and always more room, raising
    its vaults,
diminishing the piers, until the churches could no longer stand
    like this one.
We were all looking up, and looking up was a sepulchre for the spirit.
Our spirits were space and time made perceptible to the heart
and our bodies were the knowledge that Heaven was never like this.
If I were a medieval peasant mother bereaved of my one and only
    child,
here in this roseate but gloomy light like that of infancy
I would see my lost baby playing with the Christ child
in the capacious lap of the Queen of Heaven,

high and intangible over the agitation of prayer.
I would memorize Her expression more clearly than that of my
      mother—
carved in stone, in glass, ivory, gold, enamel, wax,
she would be as multitudinous as the ice stars of winter
or summer's cicadas sawing away at the little silences
to bring earth's pilgrim listeners to their knees;
as familiar as the cold stream where I washed my family's shirts,
the stones where I beat the living water out of them,
beat out every joy and sorrow and impregnation and bearing forth,
and my heart filled and flushed with the flock's blood
would understand instinctively the cruces of architecture,
how the necessity of light to ritual converted walls to windows,
how arches were raised and raised till churches could no longer
      stand
and the last chisel dropped and rang unheard in the transept of
      Common Sense—
but I would have to be reborn a tourist blinking in the sun
for there to be the ermine fields and reapers with steel-toothed stairs
and the distant hills, and the stone sheds transformed by disuse
into flowerpots for oaks and hawthorn, and one wheat storage house
that bears a painting of a flaming orange the size of a train tunnel,
and stands of cypresses writhing like columns of smoke
from staked infidels torched to traceries of fire and sparks and ash
because religious gloom always needed more and more light.
I saw a child commandeer a plastic Shuttlecraft through cathedral
      shadow
while a pigeon landed on Paul's Romanesque head to the North
and a cloud towed its shadow through stone
all before my eyes had yet adjusted to the noon.
The end will be all light as after our train to Chartres left the tunnel
and under the tidal fields, beneath a stand of cypress quills
one scarecrow up to his empty trousers in green wheat
brandished a banner of aluminum foil in the next world.

The train had borne us out of the tunnel darker
than any room our mothers ever dreamed of sending us to,
into an unsought light like that inside the skull of a slaughtered
    pig—
wondering how the gloom had gone so spectacularly stained by sun-
    light,
where the light was going at the speed of mercy.

Happiness

After Leonard Gardner and John Huston

If we become happy by saying we are happy
why don't we say it more? Why
when you say it does the cantina freeze,
even the cigarette smoke? The moment

alone is happy? Everything is simply
what it is in the idle moment
the old Mexican cook who was never young
pours you thin coffee? Smiles? You,

a boxer, say to your only friend,
a younger boxer who barely knows you,
maybe everyone is happy. He, barely concealing
his unconcern for what you are

behind the words you slur, agrees, if only
to make you happy. To make you leave him alone
to his relative lack of sadness, and he
agrees to stay, talk, then there's nothing

more to say. The quiet leads you
out among the smell of orange trees
and buses. Through pin-oak netting
a neon ad burns. All words say *need*

and boy do you need to be happy. You need
this doorway to piss blood in. No one
to tell you not to fight. The cobblestones
to stumble home across. But this is a movie,

this is a poem about a movie, and you
are nothing either way, and even
in the book you're not even nothing,
only the idea of nothing, nothing having

the right to happiness. And in bed,
the bare bulb burning on your strength, the happy
noise ascending from the sidewalks is so much
ringing in your ears, and having been

with a friend doesn't mean you are happy
or even if you were what could you do about it?
It only means that happiness gave
up a little before you did,

that the hope you more or less
maintain must look forward upon
its diminishing, and in time
lack even the heart to say good-bye.

Godlessness

We spectators, purely superfluous, rake with curiosity
our eyes across the hell the Yaqui boys look out from feigning panic,
the submissive flesh stretched across their bulldozer skulls,
and as they run the gauntlet of temporary stands,
the gray shifting rows of flowers we are in moonrise, is it our fault
we enjoy ourselves? What we know of their trials is what we see.
Since this is true the surfaces come clean of personality:
as the chapayekas storm the church to exorcise the baby Jesus
the church doors fly apart, women throw flowers
and angels spurred on by godparents rush out and thrash the backs
of the chapayekas with sticks, and when the flowers hit them in the
    face
they stagger just as they do when they hear holy words,
topple like drunks off the cliff of a religious buzz-on.
The enemies of Christ are sent to hell and it seems beautiful to us—
the angels of our own chaste skepticism,
we watch the antique moonlight embalm them with our amazement
and know their ritual thankfulness will not retrieve
the choking stars as they drift and rasp in the darkness
or the cottonwood leaves quaking, twisting into the gutters of wind
as their share of agony transforms them into
engines that pull the branches a little closer to earth,
then break down under the arc lights' sulfur glare.
Evil takes hold of the cringing outdoors, and the moon mists
with its own blue ring and the bonfire ash, and the human promise
is one coral cluster of papier-mâché masks
balancing the moonlight on a featureless sheen,
only the questioning brows stand out with the last
berserk mutter of individuality.
An effigy of Judas stuffed with fireworks
explodes into aerial blossoms for the sheer fantastic hell of it,

smoke outlasting flesh as if the earth would end
the way it began, without having consulted our genius,
till the apocalypse itself shallows into an everyday
timeless litter of breezes,
confetti and dust scudding along in brief rifts
that break like the heart into troublesome whirlpools of color,
while a small angel who slept all night on the church floor
folds a blue blanket and rubs her eyes,
not knowing in whose blood she wakes
or whose hand it is that touches the face that is hers
without destroying it. She looks at me
an instant, as if we had both looked up from the same
terrible story and saw each other momentarily,
and all the tangled confetti exhaled by the mystery,
and the blanket she folds and whatever star she wishes she were
in the trees behind her before sunbreak,
and all the stars that reach across the nothingness
with so much gloom of the first moment
are too brief to turn away from.

Old World Light

Right on schedule, one century behind,
The little bird on William Wordsworth's cuckoo clock
Emerged from Time Itself, a home, to cuckoo.
Even at midnight

You could clearly hear noon. And yet not even
In sunny Grasmere did any light come free,
Each homely chunk of coal was a commodity
Time Itself paid for;

Sufficient unto the night were the miners down below.
Together underground William and Dorothy go—
They who paid a Light Tax on their ninth window.
No place like home, though.

The benches fly backwards, the newspaper readers,
As if they'd always been left behind so far
And what they were reading no one remembers,
Wheezing old men pulled

Straight into Nothingness which is not yet filled—
New islands of light in the Tube pounding past us,
People on platforms, years of practice, stare where
Our train is no more

So why do we care when the door accordions open
To some total stranger's paradise without us?
The angels of our century are hideous,
Brushing against us—

This is as close as we get to blessedness.
Maybe in some last judgment of impending closeness,
Hands flat against glass, we'll smash through such light as
Futures all blackness;

But now each hand dusted with faery liver spots,
Each unlovely untied shoe, each overcoat
Striking a match, shaking dark a single face
Seems far away yet.

Slow Train North

After I. B. Singer

A postwar full moon, gauzed in bandages, stares into train windows.
The trees and the steaming rivers have stopped pounding backwards,

and a Yiddish scholar wakes chilled on God's idea of a train
halted on its tracks by God's idea of a snowdrift.

Stars come on like townlights seen from concentration camps.
Here in the dining car where businessmen grind out their figures,

the scholar is waking and red and black numbers are falling.
He feels like throwing his lecture out the window

with its Auschwitzes, its Treblinkas, their fairy-tale outbuildings.
His soul, not one to put up with the cold, asks his body,

could you please put on your coat, dear, before the world ends?
The scholar slumps in a train's wicker chair as the Sea of Nectar,

then the Sea of Tranquillity, then the Sea of Madness tear free
from some last snow cloud three-quarters gone to truth.

Suddenly the machinery of the night shrieks like time itself,
the train lurches north, toward Montreal, the rusted ties hold,

row after row of ghosts light cigarettes far outside the window
and fly above ghost cornfields on wicker seats.

The last drunken businessmen rise from their unsteady tables.
Night will snuff the lanterns of their faces one by one

and put them all to bed behind curtains on steel strings,
and for a long sleepless time the Ocean of Storm will ascend

to another universe where there are no businessmen altogether,
no contained light of a dining car, no bright silverware,

no scholar scarcely listening to the disembodied talk,
no yellow trees pounding past him without so much as his glance,

and no snow to fall out of nowhere all alien and mute and new,
then flow with the steaming rivers all in the wrong direction.

After the Vision of a Storm Cloud, 31 July 593 B.C.

(Ezekiel)

No peace. All prophecies were lies. A steam rose from the Chebar
to mummify each thing that creeped, the woman with an earthen

pot of bee's balm on her head, the grasshopper. Then sun,
and the shadow of the grasshopper stretched across the burning road.

The wheels had spun as long as his silent sigh held his mouth open,
till a train of camels had broken the spell. Another ordinary dawn,

and the silhouetted merchant leading them across the horizon
seemed as recollected Self, a breath of earth, or one of the slaughtered

Ezekiel once addressed as *mother, father, wife*. Such ghostly coinage.
Silverings, shekels, talents, drams, denaria, the worthless mite—

the gold become brass, the sun a canker on the firmament's azure
    shoulder.
Summer had lit the olives green, each leaf a stepping stone

to God and still no peace, only the spoked shadows
from the wheels of a passing dung cart, its mizzle of camel droppings,

then the voice of God that is God's absence, glory's rushed departure—
a voice returning as the seldom of rain returns: when it feels like it.

A scroll unrolled out of that voice, a hiding place for honeyed words,
the Chebar at the bottom of the scroll. Within and without

rattled the river reeds. A crane stuck the ice pick of its neck
into the chevroned currents and pulled out a fish dripping river light.

Ezekiel ate the scroll dripping honey, he ate all history,
he ate the sun itself and still the banks of the Chebar shone

quicksilver. Then the voice of God eating into air
told him to take a tile made of sunlight and shadow and straw

and shape a dwarf Jerusalem. Grasshoppers scoured the city walls.
A barley cake baked from the dung of a swaybacked cow

stood as the temple. Out of which maggots ate their way
and waited for wings of trout-silver twilight sheer as a snail's sigh.

A strand plucked from his brow placed in a doll's clay hand,
the priest's. One pinpricked drop of blood upon a pebble,

the altar. That is more like it. Rose petals hoisted on thorns
for Nebuchadnezzar's tents. And the scales of a fish

he spittled upright on the dust, hand over hand he set them,
shields of the tribes of Babylon, and in the roar of the Chebar

they sparkled like evening gowns. Pine needles for spears,
cicada carapaces for chariots, a flutter of a bantam feather

to set the wind upon parapets manned by mosquito skeletons.
Each of forty dawns his eyelids rose, a bloodshot vision over camps.

Each night for forty days when twilight fell, his silver stubble
shone as stars. And when he clapped his hands

the city trembled, and when he coughed, a pestilent squall
swept through the city gates—two mussel shells—and when he stopped

the nightlife breathed easy and stumbled through twisted streets.
One tear for the fleas to kneel to their starveling reflections,

one pared fingernail to scythe the wheatfield of a moon-calf's hair,
and every night while Ezekiel slumbered an orb-weaver spider

launched a bridge above the Assyrians and the Israelites,
above the Serbs and Muslims, above the many lost tribes of Hittites

and the moneyed tribes of Switzerland and the starved tribes of
    Somalia,
erecting first the bridgeheads, then hawsers across the heavens

to connect the exiled stars, walking back and forth
till the hubs radiated outward into a heavenly wheel of dew,

at dead center, a housefly gift-wrapped in gossamer—
the orb weaver brought down its spittled architecture each dawn

and this widower woke a little more crazy with lies.
The vulture shadow of his hand passed over his very own citied gloom.

And if a third of us should scatter as beard hair to a slight breeze
and another third be incinerated as a handful of chest hair,

each strand extinguished in a single gasp to the very end of sight,
we the other third can still drown in the river.

Behind barred windows in cities fanning toward the seas,
each god in the chambers of imagery is a little crazy,

but the dew is a dew of light without walls or heaven or country.

iii

Raptors

How strange it is these eagles seem so small,
like someone's aging father and mother. It's because
they're caged behind chicken wire, a browned Christmas tree
to shit on, white down matted against the wire
and flocking the Christmas tree as if these raptors were
the harbingers of winter all spring.
And I would tell you this and how these two eagles
look bleaker than sometimes our parents do when they turn to us
the hunched, loquacious sadness of their backs,
but some mood plays havoc on your face, you seem to be
anything but the near thing you are. So when
you wave to me from the other side of the cage
it's almost as if you wave to me from your very own planet Earth—
in these dark woods where even introspection seems evasive,
forever mooring us to our botched intentions,
whatever feeling comes over your face steps across
an Acheron of its own making.
Here where we push ourselves into each last frown or smile
and fall through this joy to which there seems no bottom,
the male grips a slung strand of rope
while the female swooshes in a curtain call toward the opposite end
with a rat's tail like a shoestring hanging from her beak,
then shrieks her *cac cac cac* out of almost nothing we could rue—
but I am afraid the eagles have their own theories of joy,
that to these two black angels
whom not even Dante could engage in talk, joy has talons
and two wings that can appear from almost nowhere in the sky,
barely rousing the world below in a shuddering wind,
joy that would join the raven feeding on roadkill
washed in exhaust and memorized mouthful
by mouthful and burned away by rain—

joy shrugging into depths no ray can reach,
joy of the ghastly realm the captors love to hate,
joy incarcerated if it has to be for its own
broken-winged welfare, caged and waiting and parental
joy we never feel at home in, joy at the ethereal blood
the slaughterhouse of a sunset had been hoarding,
joy at every outcry gone beyond recall,
joy at almost nothing
that could ever speak to us clearly,
joy at whatever eats away our hearts.

Black Storm

What's wrong with you, what's wrong with everyone
is what I want to know, but then the question
shatters in the distant stratospheric clouds piling up
lightning on the horizon. What's wrong with you is going to get worse
than merciless when I reach you with news of your mother's death—
just woken by your brother's call, 4 A.M., the streets still
as vacant as a parking lot built on the moon,
I hurry to rip you off the butcher's hook of sleep.
Someplace under the stars that float above like streetlights
strung by an idiot, under the sober streetlights below,
some Harley engine turns over to an official fuck-the-world.
Then streets flash off and on like an empty dance floor,
two headlights through the downpour
traveling toward one sad or happy conclusion.
The only news of where we will have been lashes the houses
and calls the steel-wool clouds across the knife of the horizon
to wear away the very edge of the known world,
until the streetlights all the way to the Astrodome go
superfluous because the first stroke of lightning
begins to believe in understanding just when it is
gone—like that, like a mother—forever out the window—
and me almost knocking the door down and you and Leah afraid
I'm either out of my mind with drink or just out of my
terrible little phone booth of a mind.
Then the shape of a grown man stupidly sobbing—
your sorrows become your very own this electric night
only so they can survive, for there's no place
like the present for survival. Suddenly my memory
is standing in the middle of a gigantic silence in Austin
without even the slightest question to make me wonder
what made me happy like that,

looking down at the public swimming pool and wanting
to stare forever down at the swimmers,
their backs to the sun in a park where aluminum canoes
were stacked in rows like sardines in the grass.
Where insects skimmed a quiet as breakable as any surface
into concentric circles dying to be each other,
the lake was pocked with zeros of realization
and each zero confined nothing but the
insane necessity of having a past.
So what was I to do but walk down to the water,
the marges dusted with yellow pollen,
and clear with a twig one wavering chink in solitude,
that old-fashioned word for telling the world
to go to hell with its cures for want and insecurity.
In the naked world below our less manageable kingdom,
fingerlings in clairvoyant schools studied a Mercurochrome confluence
where the brightest absolution was cold and twilit
and day was night, and difficulty ease.
The fingerlings clear of water healing behind them—
what were they trying to stay ahead of,
bigger, more dangerous mouths, or the lack of something,
something we must find our little ways to
before what overcomes us is our own lives?
Now we sit together and I can't think of a thing to feel.
One day this storm will be a ghost waving its dark tangle down,
bombed limbs grasping phone wires, sidewalks matted green,
fresh twigs camouflaging row on row of car tops,
kids walking across the vegetable streets as if across the tops of trees,
one day we are farther away from each other than ever sitting so close,
but in that memory I could never invite you to I keep seeing
the oaks elbowing their way into sunlight,
to the one deafening noise behind
this quiet that nothing speaks,
where you shoulder your way into the little

refrigerator light of grief
where you could be alone
and the difference between night and day
is not as extravagant as anyone imagined,
and rain could fall
like we were falling upward into the storm.

The Mist Nets

In the recurrent dream I tell you in the withdrawn beeches
so it can't hurt me, our dead friend, laid out on the steel table,
her breasts blue from the light of the electrocardiogram,
has her sternum sawed open again and again, a gaping bear trap,
the surgeon's gloved hands cradling her lungs—she'd never know
    her masked deliverers.
Their shadows writhe and twist upon tiled walls, as in a net.
Suddenly it's summer all summer long and we're watching
this pond where the green frogs twang,
engines stamped with little red tattoos, their turret heads
encased by chloroplasts, noosed tight by duckweed
—that microscopic lily too small to houseboat a family of gnats—
up to their visionary eyes in scum, they have to see
what they are hiding from, they have to see the faint mosquitoes.
I'm sure singular grief's like that, the starved
cesspool of it, its blood-gorged prey, the way
on summer nights it fucks itself into an elegiac frenzy.
And each new moment blows against the mist nets
leaves and birds caught upside down or sideways
for whom the world goes awry and trees leaf
downward into blue—three cedar waxwings,
three toffee-colored shuttlecocks so staid they seem
dreamed up along with this net too close to being nothing.
There in the hammock of invention slung across eternity,
in the shifting yet not shifting veil of want weaved
of strands of forgetfulness, their wings won't open,
they creak a little, like stuck doors—next to nothing
in you puts a hand to the marges of a pool
and now you have no face down there below our feet, below our
    sleep and our insomnia.
I don't believe in angels, trying to write about the underworld

is like trying to write about writing—
how can you when it shouldn't be this way, this isn't the morning
    the faithful dreamed of,
rubbish sunlight piled up everywhere,
this isn't heaven and these aren't cherubs but
three wedge-head waxwings cocking their heads because
every unintelligible and every awkward gaff and miscalculation
strains against entanglement made more fast by hope,
consenting to nothing,
not even the snares of our unfathomable care.

Reading Willa Cather

1

Before the next page turns it's already
chilly on the prairie,
the moment the light climbs all by itself
from the ponds and the grass.
The prairie birds find their places,
but a single gull circles a pond,
sees the windowlight, comes
right up to it.
Because the cold night won't let go
what was all ocean once,
it must think it sees a boat,
tired enough to try to take
residence in a
mistake.

2

Beyond all we know of the past
our mistakes about it have overcome us,
and it's one little night in one little year,
1962,
in Hastings, Nebraska. If a deer
were to look up from the salt lick
steaming deep in the wind-blown woods,
one of the few townlights huddled
in the spars of the pines
would be us.
We would be the pinprick
of that old folk's home
where my father unfolds a Swedish flag

for my great-grandmother.
She touches the heavenly star
she wishes she were,
but the light is only cloth.
When my father folds the flag,
he folds up the one last mistaken
memory of her country,
and hides it away.

3

How is it we can put down the most
comfortless stories in the world
and look out the window,
unless I have found an altogether stranger sight:
a father's back breaks water
and a kid on the board
wearing flippers and a face mask
is the jewel of his mother's attention,
she saying careful honey
careful with a baby
wrapped in a towel
until almost
invisible in her arms.

4

You can put your hand to the window
and touch the night and not destroy it,
or you can refuse to look up from your book
in which the night is just as indestructible—
Ivar the crazy Swede
walks barefooted all night across the grass
somewhere between the asylum and the church,

the children returning from their visit to him
hide under the hay in the wagon,
and though it's just about dawn,
the eldest daughter braces
a lantern firm between her feet
while the wagon rattles down
a shoestring highway the snow-on-the-mountain
has not healed yet.

Bottomland

The pleasure boats are tied to the docks
                like flowers snapped from their stems.
        Some writer of fairy tales should untie them
                and let each drift without
                        motive or passenger,
        and even let the ropes drift loose like snakes
                        without any hunger,

and write the sun so bright down through the water
                none of the tadpoles
        will ever sleep again,
                and all the water babies will begin to talk,
                        and drive their natal cares away
        by gossiping of the bright world above—
                        where there are cares so tall

their heavy shadows sink right through the stream.
                My friend waves to his daughter
        waving back from under the beeches,
                they are making a funny game
                        out of distance,
        and if in our sudden happiness the three of us feel our limits
                        no more than a fish

whose lateral lines extend touch into the shallows,
                what harm to burst our boots and lose our hats
        and lose our ribs and shrink our brains and grow our jaws out,
                and hang about in a dirty stream with speckled trout
                        and stickleback, and not believe
        one blinding word from the breathing world,
                        even if it is true?

We could go clean below the shallows of our best intentions
                    to where there's not the least
            bit of cloth on our backs
                and fishhooks tied
                        by so weak a thread
            they have broken free and sunk to the streambed—
                        a barbed alphabet—

the rest is the rust of afterthought and doesn't exist,
                    and is deafening.
            So this sweet confusion beneath the pond's slow eye
                would seem threatless
                        if we didn't know better, if childhood hadn't
            broken out crying the truth after all
                        that things complex and quick

are slowed by air and gravity to cares colder
                    and darker the deeper you go:
            till down is away and the depths are speechless and shallow,
                and far below the surface ease of sorrowful recall
                        the very speckled trout that make the sand dance
                    reels
            seem ruthless as the new broom of the breeze
                        that remembers to sweep the hourglass
                    spider

from its insupportable bridges
                    into the cool clean spotless Ever After All.
            When my friend kills a cigarette, the smoke
                escapes from his mouth long after
                    he stops coughing,
            his blue breath drifts so far
                        into the present

the future stops existing—
his daughter is almost brutally quiet,
and there will be more of her quiet without
our even having listened for it,
it hasn't even fully begun,
her first best cleanest thoughts already lap
too quietly to make a fairy tale.

So when he hoists his daughter over a stream too wide
for her to step over,
she sees me look at her as if she's a baby cloud
or the laugh of an otter, or the hoot of an owl
or the green caterpillar
who lets herself down from the boughs
by a silk rope

only to haul herself back into the trees, rolling up her rope—
the instant she sees me watching her
she looks at him and me like we were nuts
and turns into a little girl again
because all along she would do so,
as if all of it had already happened,
this almost storyless past.

Natural History

Rows of finches all strapped like the murderers
of gnats, mayflies, and mosquitoes that they were,
breast after yellow breast in strict finch witness,
brothers and sisters

behind glass cases in the Field Museum,
claws curled into little balls around nothing at all—
Mrs. Dunning led us through this underwater
glow called the Bird Room,

her giggling first graders, the little clients of her
untroubled guidance, though what could she teach us?
That fluorescent light was somehow timelessness,
a knowledge as brainless

as the skull of the limp-wristed tyrannosaur.
Our teacher was now pointing at this skyscraper
with vertebrae that made a crazy escalator
up to a steamshovel

jaw that scooped up nothing but a lot of air.
We drew to it as infants to a mother,
we cowered under it, it towered over our
time in its swamplight.

What could have pulled us from this Mesozoic sight
but the marvelous gift shop? I bought a kit,
a plastic guillotine complete with wicker
basket to catch the

aristocratic head again and again.
This kit was somehow what I set my sights on.
All crime would be punished again and again
in my revolution.

And yet I felt sorry for the tyrannosaur
or the almost inhuman sight of our bus driver
exhaling dead smoke, green dashlight smeared all
over his glasses,

as deep into Daylight Savings as he could wait,
embalmed like a mummy in the winding sheet
of his exhalations, removed from us,
unthought of, yet there—

The engine coughed on, headlights drilled through water-down.
And there I sat, the little executioner
watching the snowflakes strange and vagrant before
sidewalks destroyed them,

our footprints still trudging up the museum
steps without us or any ancient teacher.
Streetlights were haloed in snow's stupefaction—
angelic, it glistened

all the way down from heaven to Chicago.
And skyscrapers half-vanished in a white cloud
and one of them was where my father worked
all through my childhood.

Big Language

In every sense of every word I'd roam
Past each streetlight waiting out each sunset,
And walk the dark consent inside me home.

Behind my back, clouds rolled away like foam,
And school became a thought, and every thought
In every sense of every word would roam.

And every syllable became a schoolroom,
And every feeling, one big happy thought
Walking the dark consent inside me home,

Past the country club where parents swam
Or soaked in those sunny days their money bought.
In every sense of their every word I'd roam

Till their laughter lifted far above their kingdom,
Gone just like smoke beneath the sun that set,
Leaving my dark consent without a home—

For I was just a cloud above their kingdom.
Big language stuttered one more idiot,
Who every sense of every word would roam
Until he made his dark consent his home.

Cruising

Four of us piling into the Camaro,
we glided above the asphalt into outer space,
past cornstalks tossing up their scarves in rows,
past paperweight cows

holding down the hills our headlights threw out.
We drank ourselves into a girlless paradise,
we laughed away the female in us all but
raped her in private.

And what a pal dog the future was back then,
bounding ahead of desire in and out of the fog,
gone wherever alleys lead when they are gone,
a bark without its dog.

Now each desire's a prolonged adolescence.
Beyond my wife's ghost outside the jet window,
beyond the wing's steel tilt, the northern lights throw
bodiless serpent-slough-

flashings the blue-green color of arctic ice.
Below us, upstate New York towns dash through clouds
loose as sauna steam with lights as bodiless.
Celestial stewardesses

walk by on air. And her ghost almost smiles away
the world below, and unforgotten tedium;
this, or our boredom opens like a heaven
we will come back from.

Negative Confession

I razor-slit three hits
of Emerald Pyramid
for five of us, and through
a hairline crack in the dusk, pure space had broken through
with everything we ever
meant to be tincturing the fire-pond crimson.
One afterlife and the next
seeping away, even the one
called Shame. Phantasmal,
unremembering, we all tried to act
as if everything were normal,
while the windowed end
of the world began again,
a few last blackbirds
thrown across the cornfields
like something torn from earth,
beyond our cool quiet
and the skeletal sycamores,
into the orphanage
called Twilight.

That October sunset
looked us all easy in the eyes
and told us we would never die
except to dread and wonder.
Twenty years later, if telling
resurrects, then listen O my heart, for we
did not want a peaceful afterlife.
In *The Egyptian Book of the Dead*
at judgment the heart is placed
on a brass balance

and weighed
against the Feather of Truth.
This is when, if you are lucky, your heart refuses
to testify against itself.
You never asked your servants to work
past dawn,
nor caught fishes with bait
of their own bodies, nor
set the homeless on fire.
You never cursed your luck
except in shame,
to yourself.

I think I am afraid our best
exalted intentions
wouldn't outweigh a feather.
We held in smoke till the seahorse exhalations
swam around the Chinese lantern
while the oaks,
brazen with blackbirds,
sang us down from heaven
twenty years ago.
Their shadows threw themselves past us
as if we were stubble.
Where in the afterlife
of saying so
are my almost friends? O my dumb heart,
why confess to you?
Could you ever
lie for me, lay me down cold,
lie down in a jar of wine
and still refuse
the safety of dying?

The Human Brain

They say that memory is electrical,
along with the constant arrival of our sorrow,
that bells and meat, thunder and lightning
are mirrored by molecular learning inside the cell,
and every time we read a book or hear a lecture
little bumps on our dendrites swell and explode.
They say the gas station I reach with my friend
in a Ford Galaxy appears as a cellular alphabet
emitting a shower of neurotransmitters
across the spaces between axon and dendrite.
That even our wish for the gas station to be there
is like looking through a diamond of calcium ions.
The gas station unfolded a kind of black rose
of oily light wherein we sat feeling protected from the theories of night,
though I thought I could hear the dirt
from his hometown drop out of his laughter,
and so the past sieves through us endlessly.
Potassium expelled as sodium rushes in.
This is my only memory of this friend
and what it means has faded with why we stopped
or why better than his face I remember
some kind of bug flying into an insect zapper,
tiny executions which made us laugh

and now are stored in a sprawling sequence of neurons
as forms of sensitization and habituation
in cells each built like the old Philco radio
I remember my mother waxing poetic on
without this practiced detachment.
We killed an elf owl that night with a headlight,
stumbled out of our car and saw it on the road.

Head missing and still it was there, triggering
so many engrams and ion channels—none of which
constitutes this elf owl unable to think itself
back to the creosote one of us pitched it in.
And what I want my subatomic indifference to tell me is
how the sight of it could have made so
cozy a nest in some cerebral treetop of
these singing nerves, but the nucleotides
aren't saying anything even if they know.
I may never find a way out of this desert.
While a new snow blows across Lake Michigan from Wisconsin,
I'm watching the brain of Sergei Eisenstein
in a jar of formaldehyde on TV. A crass
60 Minutes story on a very literal Soviet Braintrust:
Stalin's, Nijinsky's, Gorky's. And all

the unfinished scripts of Sergei Eisenstein
lost in the dark woods of his neural brainmeat—
sliced thin as mica to put under the microscope.
We all remember the scene in Potemkin
where through sheer neglect the baby carriage
drops down an infinite case of marble stairs
there's no way back from seeing or believing.
The sight of the baby's face is what we remember beyond revolution—
blessed by the benediction of the lens,
that transparent carnation you could be sucked
into and be preserved and hurled by, as a blue shaft
of light above the faces of the moviegoers.
If I turned from the afterlife of the narrative up there on the screen
I saw neon exit signs eating up the dark.
This was before my long-gone friend and I
stared at the elf owl that got in the way
of our car and turned out to be no tragedy.
Its neck steamed little seahorse wisps of steam

there's also no way back from seeing or believing.
It seems almost unconscionable to talk about
this sequence of events as agonistic
and antagonistic molecules without which there
would be no black branch of a desert highway,

no all-night gas station and no frying bugs.
The moon looked like a prop watching over us.
My friend's arm, tattooed with an anchor,
slung indifferently over an inert steering wheel
while insects fried out loud: so many laughable
electrocutions constitute the past, which is a desert night.
Even remove is a lightning storm of synaptosomes,
without which no one is sitting in the movies,
no one is slicing the brain of Sergei Eisenstein
and no one's unfilmed wishes spend so many
dark years afloat in freezer light.
Then the knife sinks to the bottom of genius.
It's practically snowing genius tonight, the roads outside
are lined with scree of plowed snow, new snow
oozing to old in this bottomless night.
And each fat drop the icicles turn out
is practically a moral imperative
to stop thinking of memory as punishment
or theory as anything but shame.
No process is too minuscule to mourn.

Heraclitus, Fragment 16

There's a lot of night to skim over.
By dusk the lake is prematurely night
as if this half of earth can't wait
to receive its portion of the dark, and we
are what's acutely wrong with this picture,
we and our borrowed craft are out of place here,

our failed bait sinks to a junkyard beneath the hull.
Slicing through the mist, the gasdock glow
frees us to the growing dark from tiny lightbulbs
behind their Lilliputian windows—
numbered spools paying out the integers of cost,
soon the engine cutting quiet with a sound

almost as rueful as a death rattle.
Everything you look at when awake
is death, a now defunct philosopher said.
Which means my friend is a corpse;
his hand still on the throttle with the memory
of so small a purpose is less than bloody pointless,

as is whatever watches him let out a cord
run through the pointed snouts and out the gills
of one pike and one walleye. Blue unliving nylon
cord insinuates itself beneath the abysmal
leaflike veins of the ripples and I must be sleeping—
nothing looks remotely dead, even the two fish trying

to swim like there's no tomorrow as long
as night has no bottom, no ghoulish shore.
Only the stars go under without hurting

themselves, without our sinking, without
our even consenting to let them sink
till the tidal scrolls of a gasdock's lap and hiss

unravel into a night without cease.

Paradise, Michigan

True, astronauts can see the wakes ships leave
and just as true the birds can see the stars
and it is also true that stars and fireflies
are equiponderant to human sight;
both sink into our very torment, our very
love of the turmoil we are to each other,
but only stars sink upwards from Superior.
The stars are nothing to the fireflies.
Both are prehistoric, both require night
to turn them on, both appear and reappear,
both hold one sky in common as do the
living and the dead, both strafe this dark thing
that sleeps in us all day until the sun falls
and the towns that we sleep in seethe anew
—as when all the lights in the house are burning.
Your let your fingers brush my face the way moths
bang the screen door of this bright motel room
all they want. They're all the same, all
white as the moon and all wings till the last
little finger of your touch is everywhere,
and we awake to look across a graveyard
which is no graveyard at all, but Whitefish Bay.
Below a corrugated iron pier twelve miles
from Paradise,
300 plus corpses are out there under water;
all these ships went down too perfectly
and yet this planet's crowded as it is,
and we don't have a clue as to how to make
the world dance to our love, so we dream
far into another summer of consent.
We heard two hundred dollars puts your name

upon a star, we actually talk about it.
Need says whatever comes into our heads,
need invents a telephone book of stars,
holocausts a dial tone away.
We need motels, the numbered doors of sleep,
we need the slow cat of the water's lap and leer
to slush against no piers money can buy
a name for, we need money more and more,
we need our need to pay outside so far
it blinds us with the light of where we are.
Need is what we believe, and we believe it all,
we believe the bottom right hand of the moon
to be precise and ruthless to the very edge
of where precision ends, and where consent begins—
cars topping the sludge of Michigan's great dunes,
the glowworms of illuminated beech trunks,
and in the motel sleeping couples who
consent to private dreams, whereas the
waking consent to one world in common.
No two can see the same star even once
and so we dream of squandering two hundred dollars
to name one star, one strife so far away
distance seems a blinking toy.
This firefly upon your shirt is worth
a hundred billion stars named after us.
This firefly above the planet Mars
despises dying way up here or way down
there all the same, and if we stare at stars
to keep them distant or to bring them near
is all the same, and it is all the same
to sit out on a beach as it would be
to turn back to our motel room, its
tiny soaps and cheerfully logoed matchbooks.
If day and night are one, if Heraclitus,

guardian of the living and the dead,
has gone the way of light-years into night
and if it's death for soul to become water
and life for water to ascend to fire,
then if it's all the same I'll stare
a little longer as the good philosophers
weeping or laughing must have stared because
weeping or laughing all the same is fire,
the dead lucidity and the living ignorance,
the stars gone under without sinking us,
the love-drained bioluminescing fireflies
gone asleep in the grass. . . . The dunes step off
soundless behind us and eat the stars.
Brave little lights are snuffed out everywhere.

Brotherhood

Some nights there's so much of it
even the gray winds blow with
direction, but not that night.
I climbed up from the ditch bank
toward the ruby lights from the
elevators of summer wheat,
jewels fixed above some town's
distantly useless houselights.
A rain starting, I crawled up
beneath a chance overpass,
a rural route for a ceiling.
Too far below to drench me,
water sizzled under tires.
Farther below than Dante
a man ran out of the rain,
a white dress shirt soaked through
to his undershirt, his suit
he picked up for nothing from
some thrift shop he found in hell,
Wichita, whichever—
he bore the spooked look of a
dog shut out in a storm, left
to its little futile truth,
till the instant our eyes met,
then he ran back into the flood
before that face drowned us both.

The Mysteries of the End

1

Out of thin air archangels have materialized wings, beak, and hollow
    bones
to land from on high as starlings into the cemetery catalpa—
burning like strings of black Christmas bulbs, or pilfering earth
    for worms
among the obelisks. In the highest branches that hunch out of roots
    is a peregrine,
its right eye on the starling that scavenges with the patience of saints
and the steadfastness of the homeless, and there in the blue
    swimming pool
of tree shadow, talons wrap around the starling's chest and the beak
    goes agape,
claws without grasp like the stems of eaten grapes, crocuses
    springing,
some body's being eaten, the instant closing like the eye of some
    roadkill.
I'm here with my wife who can't pass a cemetery without stopping—
the one in Maui with the cracked porcelain faces of Japanese
    immigrants
staring out of the calm of some photographer's studio somebody
    remembers;
the famous one in Paris where a bunch of yellow roses tied with kite
    string—
the blossoms might ascend into the lumbering clouds that won't
    survive the afternoon—
brighten the imposing tonnage of blackstone that marks the bones of
    Proust;
or this towny one that seems so momentary a wakefulness,
a starling pinned to grass, ants crawling all over the unbloomed
    peonies

because only promise may be sugary, and the keeper's children
 downstreet
from these starry birds to whom the trees are married everyday—the
 world has ended,
the children in heaven, rolling their hula hoops over the under-
 ground lovers,
their three-legged dog running around the side of their house and
 them
calling to the dog as if the house weren't there, as if a broken dog
hiding behind the house shouldn't be broken and shouldn't be
 hiding,
as if these children could see right through their house and its living
 room
and its sofa in shambles and the snowflake doilies all the way to
 their footworn yard.

———————

Maybe the end will come as a piece of grade-B camp,
as when our Cub Scout troop went downtown to see
The Beginning of the End up there on the screen,
and grasshoppers the size of Atlas moving vans
towered over the streetlit elms of the southernmost suburbs,
antennae inclining toward the great shining Chicago,
until science saved the world from science itself—
loudspeakers set up in fishing boats off the shores
of Lake Michigan—and from the giant grasshoppers,
lured by a grasshopper mating call pitched higher
than any hearing save that of insects or God.
They slouched through the Loop, up the Wrigley Building,
over the bridge, under the El, down Michigan Avenue,
past the two bronze lions guarding the Art Institute
and right under the Prudential Building, where
my father spent thirteen years blueprinting slaughterhouses,
my father who entered his business from the bottom

and without so much as a flick of the wrist
learned to pry open a pig until it confessed
it was as starved as the rest of creation for every
filthy wake that doused the stars with industrial blood.

Grasshoppers doomed to their miniature shining city,
the camera on its tripod whirring above them,
like the wheels of Elijah's chariot—
climbing across toy cars, toy buses, a toy train track,
to float in our lake before some cameraman's assistant
plucked them out of a sandbox filled with water,
and in the background smoking cigarettes,
chewing gum, yawning, waiting for the workday if not
the very world to end, were the human forms divine,
the sad or happy extras of lesser magnitude,
from other stage sets, cowboys drinking Cokes,
angels blowing smoke rings, gorillas with their
giant heads in their hands and all the time in the world—
as if we would never step outside the theater
and be drenched in infrared and ultraviolet
cloudlight from some Golden Book of Clouds—
as if the hand which stands upon the earth
and upon the sea would never place our city
as sweet as honey into the jaws of the Scribe,
until the Everafter singes and the projector light
shines through celluloid and our city really shines
right through that scared child looking up at the screen,
grasshoppers munching the elms and streetlights
that empty their sight on the grass and see no sorrow.

Then looking backwards from the narrative
into the tortoiseshell darkness of the balcony above,
rows of watchers blown away toward what
next world the rising credits will not say

except that it won't be childhood or the movies.
The same day the world ended we found ourselves
marched into the undergloom of the Shedd Aquarium,
pressing our hands to our see-through Cub Scout selves.
Angelfish came round and round to look upon us all,
and nearly transparent spawn squirmed into the jaw
of the jawfish so as to ride out forever their instant:
in this warm-blooded allegory of absolute shelter,
which began in the movies and ended in an aquarium—
the halved beer keg, aquiline beak, and beady
centurian eyes of the hawksbill turtle,
flying, sort of, in a half-lit-up forever,
the little flashlight fish almost snuffed out
by simply having been glanced at.
Glommed onto the glass was a pink octopus,
gashes where eyes should have been, each tender
white suction cup staring at us all the way
to the tip of touch, where no touch was,
all grasp, only itself to hold, already home.
Our grayling shapes thronged and huddled beating the glass—
seen through the depths of the tank by some
total stranger, we must have looked featureless,
unrealized, like, say, the clouded memories
of loved ones you have when you die

2

though we lived, driven back to suburbs, past
rows of houses aglow like lowered bathyspheres,
the stricken matches of streetlights and filthy
trees constructed leaf by leaf of smog, streets
oily, beneath perdition even. I was
sitting next to Spencer Poulos, from down
my street, who has long since died of leukemia,

the only Virgil of my broken dreams.
I can't remember the name of his father.
We rode the Skyway home on a Blue Bird
over Gary, we rose on concrete stilts,
we crossed the heavens into dusk and low-
slung clouds the color of industrial blood,
all those oily streets with tiny street signs
below memory, filthy locust trees.

In dreams he shows up on a broken escalator
or on the lowest ring of a shopping center.
His smile, the aspect of a smile, always
suggests this isn't the revolving door
for me, this store is overloaded with
trauma, coded lusts, unanalyzable betrayals.
Then he drifts into a crowd of shoppers
like I was the ghost, like time had sunk into
the love of mercy and the rant of love.
Then I awake. Even the dream of him
goes far below the underwater gloom
into some torpor older than recall.
My King James Bible on the reading stand.
Voices of birds like voices from a subway.
Grasshoppers in the trees and in the grass,
streetlights still on, as if the grasshoppers
needed a little more light than the dawn
to blow away, and I still see my friend.

———————

The corpse unburns, ashes slide back onto
their embers, the sobbing of the bereaved,
played backwards, murmurs as one sublime waterfall,
the rigor mortis of the seated grievers ends,
the tears climb back into their secret ducts,

the gray ghost hills exhume consenting stars,
the gravestones are loaded back onto trucks
every time I think back my dead friend.
All the human blood and human dust
and human shit stumbles back into struggle,
and long summer evenings are restored down
to the shadow of every last grasshopper
every time I think back my dead friend.
He's charring a grasshopper stuck to a wad
of gum with his looking glass from Sears,
tightening the sunlight to an ice pick,
letting all the speechless sunlight through
every time I think back my dead friend.

3

Or maybe the resurrection is only a matter of reprieve,
the way my mother came back to a hospital bed,
the faces of her passed-on loved ones jacklighting her,
and snapped out of that adamantine vision like a deer
ambling back to the shaggy living darkness of trees,
and found herself inside a body that must have seemed
remembered, old, loathsome, too ridiculous to be hers,
shrouded under crisp sheets on a steel table cold and blue,
back to the blue light through the clear polyethylene bags,
to the masked faces of deliverers never known by name,
the tiled walls perspiring, their shadows writhing
and twisting like smoke from some unappeasable fire.
Maybe even Death and Hell along with the oily streets
beneath my childhood and the insectile streets of Hollywood
will be cast as failed concepts into the lake of fire,
to die that second death as terrorized John of Patmos,
in a phantasmagoria George Bernard Shaw called
the curious record of the visions of a drug addict—

gone will be her husband swaying over her like some
tree sweeping into its own weeping reflection.
Only one moment is true, all the rest are turning, returning
around that single moment till the whole hoard lifts together
and every moment freezes like flies on flypaper,
including the one that spelled out love for my parents
in the Omaha Union Station, below the Art Deco stained-glass windows,
the pews where soldiers waited to push out to Omaha Beach.
Where the blooded moon far to the east of America might bring
to mind the blood-soaked pages of Revelations:
all that red ink meaning Christ is speaking now to the author.
It's 1943, and over the Midwest a few of 9000 Japanese fire balloons
are drifting harmless upon the jet stream, or crashing into barns,
though in the *Omaha World Herald* my father is reading,
one fire balloon has paused above Fiftieth Street and Underwood
    Avenue.
He can almost see it disappear like a taillight going down a road.
For one incendiary moment in a train station beneath the freighted
    heavens
my parents in this cathedral honoring the Industries of Meat and
    Steel
kiss forever and anon before a pew of uniformed witnesses,
and not once do their eyes open to the Gods of Industry,
the limestone bas-reliefs of laborers with oil cans and laborers with
    hammers
who seem to have risen above that first romantic instant
of more tenderness than not within the radiance of time.

4

And when the dead friends of childhood step into
the headlights of grief, whatever changed in them
we never got to know doesn't come into thought
but ducks behind trees. I'd like to start creation all over

with the same kind of hopeless modesty ghosts must have
but trying to start from scratch is like trying to hear myself
every day when I hear the guy down the street screaming
a scream from the bottom of a bottomless well.
He lives inside the School for the Disabled,
where through the windows of ministration
you can see the men and women in wheelchairs
going wherever they go, and not going far.
There in the imbecilic light of charity you can see
a fifty-year old woman in a *Star Wars* T-shirt
trying to count to three in hopeless modesty,
her hand quaking because addition shudders her.
Trying to think back the dead friends of childhood
is like trying to stare into the lightning after it thunders,
or trying to put off trying, till the guy down the street stops
screaming *hi hi hi hi hi hi hi,* endless greeting.
And when it lightnings we have seen the instant
in the field where we shall live and die,
an open playground wet to the skin,
and swingset chairs squealing empty,
neural trees asway and mental,
and a man in fuzzy slippers
crying out a welcome that doesn't take.

The Oasis Motel

I touch you like the waves admire the weirs.
It is themselves they push out from, toward what
they are a part of, and it is transportation,
and this is why palms rustle, why the moon
drops shamelessly below the horizontal
off the Gulf of Mexico, and why you, too,

are something else, and utterly familiar.
And when I turn from comfort to a fight
picking up in the outdoor bar below,
one angel has asked another if he'd like
his face pushed in on this fantastic evening—
here at the edge of our nation the ravening void

fills with his sobbing, tearless plea for mercy,
convincing me I too have dearly suffered,
I too am equally amazed at terror's
lucidity and broachable distance.
The coward angel with a bloodied face
stumbles across new silences to his car

for everyone leaves exactly when he wants to,
and the way the coastal highway freight trucks rumble
beyond all sad reproach is just too awful,
for why else would the reading lamp enclose us,
why else would your arm be thrown across
the pillow in its unforgettable journey

all the way securely to your fingers
unless the night has nothing more nor less
to do with us than some small boatlight now

heading out from shore, and where it is
is not so far from where it was, and it
is lost to sight, and it is heading forth.

Notes

"**The Suicides**"—in memory of Joe Bolton.

"**After Chartres**"—a few phrases come from Henry Adams's *Mont Saint Michel and Chartres.*

"**The Mist Nets**"—in memory of Linda Schraufnagel.

"**Negative Confession**"—takes its name from chapter 125 of *The Egyptian Book of the Dead.* This chapter consists of a prayer to be said over the body of the dead. The irresistible appeal of this prayer is that it skips over those sins all too actual and seemingly numberless, and instead elaborates on the sins, equally numberless, that the dead, in life, *did not commit.*

"**The Human Brain**"—some "facts" owing to *In the Palaces of Memory* by George Johnson.